Mel Bay Presents

Steve Kaufman's Favorite 50 Celtic Jigs and Waltzes for Mandolin

GW00838317

CD Contents

1 2 3 4 5 6 7 8 9 0

Visit us on the Web at www.melbay.com — E-mail us at email@melbay.com

Table of Contents

Steve Kaufman's Favorite Fifty (Forty-Nine) Waltzes and Jigs - Introduction

I have always been into fiddle tunes of any kind. Celtic, Appalachian, Canadian and Texas fiddle tunes have been my forte and main stay of selection because of the intensity and drive found in the tunes and the history behind them. I am very happy to bring this compilation of **Steve Kaufman's Favorite Fifty Waltzes and Jigs** to you in a format that should be easy to learn. The title implies 50 but this project came from the massive Mel Bay Book "Steve Kaufman's Encyclopedia of Celtic Tunes (MB98282)" which had 49 jigs and waltzes. I chose to keep the same number of tunes. But don't feel shorted. In all of the other "Favorite 50" books I have with Mel Bay you will find many, many tunes over the 50 mark. I am sure you will enjoy them all.

Let me give you a little background on the evolution of this book. It took about one and a half years to complete aided by friends on both sides of the water. I had been playing Celtic tunes all my life so writing a book on the subject seemed at first to be right up my alley and truly a magnificent yet enormous project. I got started in January of 1998 doing the preliminary research and writing out some tunes that I knew but it wasn't until August of 1998 that I got the real feel for the music. My family and I took a 24-day trip touring England, Ireland and Scotland. Meetings were set up through several friends in those countries where some of the finest pickers were assembled and I was able to record them and ask questions. It originally came out as **Kaufman's Encyclopedia of Celtic Fiddle Tunes For Mandolin**. This large book included 275 songs and was quite massive in weight and price. It also did not include any CDs. So Bill Bay and I decided to break the manuscript into four volumes – Hornpipes, Waltzes and Jigs, Reels A- L and Reels L-W. I was also able to record all 275 songs so now all four books are complete with CD.

I came to these afore mentioned sessions prepared with my trusty mini-disc recorder ready to record tunes and conduct interviews. The instruments at these jam sessions were often fiddles, pipers, button accordions, button harmonica, banjos and guitars. The musicians were all incredibly proficient. It gave me a feeling that every picker in the United Kingdom was world-class talent. More often than not, at the end of each inspiring and now recorded tune I would ask *"What was that tune called?"* and a typical answer would be *"It doesn't matter"*.

It doesn't matter was a phrase I heard very often. And this was a remarkable lesson. I soon learned that it really does not matter what the tunes were called. As explained to me in great detail near the end of my journey for the quest for new and interesting traditional Celtic fiddle tunes along with the titles, the tune is the tune. The tune is the important factor and the title is nothing more than something you and I can use to categorize or place the song into a slot of some kind. You use the title to specify and remember certain tunes but the title is the least important part of the tune- it's only a tag or like a post-it note.

I was at a session in Cambridge, England set up by guitarist Mark Jones, at the home of Lucy Delap and Clive Lawson. Lucy and Clive are great fiddlers and to break up the two fiddles, Lucy switches to the pipes. Lucy's sister, Mary Nugent, an incredible wooden flutist and Mark Jones were there too. The session was wonderful. I did not recognize any tunes but the music was strong and seeping with tradition and history. I was taping tunes and gathering information when I was asked to break out the guitar and "trade tunes". I tuned up and was ready to pick the next tune with my hosts when I asked Clive *"What's the chords to this one?"* and he replied (you guessed it) *"It doesn't matter"*.

This was like the final straw for this formal picker and I argued that you can't play just anything. You need to know the key and then the sub-tones that fit with the notes of the songs making up the chord structure. He then replies in a friendly and unassuming way *"It doesn't matter"*. Then in walks another picker, Andy Locker, and when he breaks out the banjo I asked what the chords were and he looked at me and said as plain as day *"It doesn't matter"*. Clive gave me a look that could cut like a hot knife through blood pudding and I was compelled to then believe him. And through this important lesson, I learned again that "It Doesn't Matter", for Celtic music anyway. Also in this Cambridge session was Hazel Fairbairn on fiddle, Josie Nugent - fiddle. I remember a funny story from that session. When I was asked to trade tunes I played one that I had learned while working on my

"Kaufman's Collection of American Traditional Fiddle Tunes For Guitar". We passed it around and Lucy picked right up on it and we played it another few minutes. Lucy then asked what it was called. I told her that we call it **"Green Fields Of America"** and she said in the sweetest Irish accent *"Oh No...... we call that '* ***There's A Hole In My Heart Large Enough To Stuff A Turnip In It'*** *"* (see the song in this book). What a great title. Thank you all for the great session and lesson.

The 'Key' is important to the tune. This tells us if the song "sounds" right when playing the notes in sequence. The chord or background harmony tones will have to match these tones somehow but when you physically attach a solid and defined chord structure to a Celtic tune you have somehow tampered with tradition. These old and traditional tunes had no chords when they were written. They were **'The Tunes'**. Any harmonies (chords) only augment the tune but they are not now or ever cast in stone. The chords written in this book are only a small example of what can be done in the background. They are only a suggestion so feel free to use what sounds best to you at the time. I was taught another lesson. Keep in mind that the guitar is somewhat new to this music compared to pipes and fiddles.

I had a great experience taping a bagpipe player in Colander, Scotland. He was a National Champion Piper who was busking at a tourist bus station in order to practice. He said his room mates didn't want to hear him all day long so he goes to the streets and makes a little (a lot of) change at the same time. He regularly performs at Sterling Castle.

A friend of mine in Dublin set up a session that explained a lot to me about Pub Sessions. His name is Ronnie Norton of Norton and Associates in Dublin. Ronnie is a great friend to music and musicians and happens to be (in mine and his countrymen's opinion) one of the greatest photographers in Ireland along with a running brilliant graphic arts business. He set up a pub session for me with several in attendance. I witnessed something all together new to me. We in America play either bluegrass style or Old Timey style. That is to say in bluegrass style everyone playing gets a solo while the rest of the jammers play rhythm or back up. Old Time play is closer to Pub Session Celtic players in that they all play in unison. Everyone plays at the same time, note for note identically so that no one is the star in the light. This is a very strong sounding way of playing music and is very enjoyable to listen to. Most of the time someone calls out a song and the one song is played for 5 minutes or so.

In the Celtic Pub Sessions they play "sets" of songs. This was one of the neatest things I witnessed. The fiddler would mutter something, put the fiddle under his/her chin look up at all the musicians and start a tune. Then after a few rounds of 250 BPM unison play, the fiddler would look up with his eyes only, as if looking over his glasses, and BOOM!, they would be into another song without a word said. Then after two to three rounds of the next tune in unison BOOM!, they would go into another tune. This author did all he could to hold on. They would go through 4 or 5 songs to the set. What a thrill- this is an exciting way to play and to beat all, these musicians were great! They get together one or two times a week at this pub for who knows how many years, and this goes on at almost every pub in the U.K.

Ronnie Norton still speaks the ancient Gaelic language and has helped in the translation of some of the tunes in this book. One in particular is called **"Muckin' O' Geordie's Byre"**. I sent Ronnie an E-mail and his reply was swift and true. He said-

"Good to hear from you and to see that the ancient art of slang translation is still of value. As we better spoken folk would say ***"Muckin' O' Geordie's Byre"*** *is properly pronounced as* ***"The Mucking Out Of Geordie's Byre"****. In which Byre means cow shed or stable and mucking out refers to an old Irish or British custom of washing and sweeping the floor of said stable after the bovine residents have soiled it. Geordie is the nickname given to a gentleman who hails from the area of England around the river Tyne and towns such as Newcastle-upon-Tyne. Muck is a colloquial noun, which broadly refers to any damp or watery dirt such as wet clay, or fresh animal manure so therefore mucking is a verb relating to the cleaning out of the aforementioned substance.*

'What it really means is "we shoveled the poop out of Geordie's cow house", but don't say that I told you. And if that's not a load of Bull then I don't know !!!!!!" And thank you Ronnie for that definitive response.

I think the two greatest experiences of the trip was getting a glimpses into the lives of the people that live and breath this great art form of music. The friends we met are hard working, honest people with strong a heritage and sense of tradition. I will always look forward to any trip back to this old world of new friends. The second greatest experience was being able to be on this glorious trip with my family. Mark and Donna (my head of Sales and Marketing and my Director/ Producer respectively) were there to enjoy the new world. Upon our return to Tennessee I asked Mark what his favorite part of the trip was and he said "staying in the land of the Castles".

Rhythm:
I have arranged these tunes and chords in standard tuning. The guitarists playing Celtic music often tune in DADGAD tuning. This means that each string is tuned from low to high E as D A D G A D. You will also note that many of the tunes written in this book are in the key of "D". By tuning in DADGAD you have the ability for lots of droning stings and pairs of fretted notes would be usually made up of a root and a fifth. See the page on chord forms that can be used other than the traditional forms used in most standard tuning guitar playing.

The rhythm can either be played with an alternating bass strum pattern or played with a free sweeping strum pattern (it doesn't matter).

Hornpipes have a loping sound to them so the one measure sweeping strum will sound like DA-da-DA-da DA-da-DA-da with accents on the down beats (the DA's) and a light up strum on the up beats (the da's).

Jigs have 6 beats in every measure so the rhythm has to also reflect this. Count over and over - 1, 2, 3, 4, 5, 6, 1, 2, 3, 4, 5, 6, 1, 2, 3, 4, 5, 6 etc. Let's make the strums with the pick hand represented by a "D" for a down strum and an "U" for the up swing. Now count the numbers again and then picture it with the strums going D U D D U D DUDDUD or you could go DxU DUD DxUDUD and yet another pattern could be DxU DxU which is again a loping kind of sound. Another pattern that I saw popular though it is very difficult to get fast is: DDU DDU DDU DDU. Whichever you chose keep in mind that

a) It doesn't matter and
b) Don't add extra beats into the 6 beat measure.

Reels/Rants. A reel is a rant so when you see that in print you'll know what we are talking about. Reels seem to be the fastest of the three main types of Celtic tunes. They would be like the USA's breakdown. These songs are generally played with alternating bass/strum patterns.

Chord Structure:
You will find that some of the chord harmonies differ from the common North American progressions. I found the different chord structures fascinating, logical and very pretty. They were just a little different than the usual I, IV, V progressions I've gotten used to in Appalachian fiddle tunes but they definitely grow on you and can be used in many other types of music.

Feeling the Timing, Lilt and Cadence of the Instrumentals:
The type of tune determines the bounce of the piece. For example the reels are played rather quickly so you won't hear much lilt even though it is there. When played correctly you will hear a long note then short one. The notes are written as straight eighths but they are technically played as a dotted eighth then a sixteenth. They will sound like DA da Da da etc. The faster you play, the less gaps you will hear between the notes but the lilt will still be there. When you play the hornpipes you will really feel and hear this dotted note play.

Key Signatures:
The key signature is supposed to reflect the scales and modes used in the song as well as the chord structure of the piece. This is not the case in this book in some instances. In some of the written materials that I used as source, the key signature (number of sharps or flats in the top left corner) did not reflect the actual key of the

song. I believe this was done in order to avoid writing in many accidentals (littering the page with many sharps and flats). The key of the song is written as **Key of __**. This is what you should go by.

Tempos and Speeds for Metronome Settings:

Here is a guide and starting point to understanding the tempos of the different types of tunes. These are not numbers and tempos that I have come up with in order to frustrate you. They represent the tempo that is comfortable for dancing. See the chart in the Understanding The Timing section for further descriptions.

Slip Jigs - a Dotted Quarter Note = 144 bpm
Double Jigs - a Dotted Quarter Note = 126 bpm
Slow Jigs - a Dotted Quarter Note = 80 bpm
Reels - Quarter Note = 225 bpm
Hornpipes - a Quarter Note = 180

In closing this introduction, I want to thank all the people throughout our journeys that helped to bring this project to life. All of our new friends in England, Ireland and Scotland. Those sessions are well etched into my memory and the friends and new faces with be with me always. Special thanks to Mr. William Bay and all the folks behind the scenes at Mel Bay Publications for publishing these works and helping to preserve so much music of all kinds.

I hope you all have a lot of fun and hours of enjoyment playing through these arrangements to some of the finest Celtic tunes that this author is aware of. Keep in mind that there are thousands and thousands of tunes so always be on the look out.

If any (reasonable) questions come up or any comments are to be made please feel free to contact me by either calling 800-FLATPIK (865-982-3808) or writing to me at:

PO Box 1020
Alcoa, TN
37701
or E-mail me at **Steve@flatpik.com**

Best always
Steve Kaufman

Play through the following exercise to get familiar with the notes and tablature. Be sure to watch out for the timing. All of the notes are hit with down swings. Play the exercise with the notes first. Check yourself with the notes chart to find where all the notes are, then go through the exercise using the tab. Play it backwards and forwards to help familiarize yourself with the notes and tab. Be sure to play it backwards and forwards. Trust me - I have my reasons.

The next few examples deal with timing. The first measure (example one) shows four quarter notes. They are all hit with a down swing. On top of each measure is a row of numbers with an "+" sign between them. When you hit the quarter notes or any notes larger than a single eighth note, they are hit with down swings on the number beats. To see how this works, count out loud 1+2+3+4+. Now hit the notes when you say the numbers. Be sure to count steadily and don't hit any note on an "+" beat. This is the proper way to hit quarter notes.

The next measure (example two) shows eighth notes. It doesn't matter whether the notes are tied or beamed together at the top or the bottom or whether they are grouped in sets of two notes or four notes. The first eighth note is always hit down and the second eighth note is hit up and so on. Count the 1+2+3+4+, hitting the first note down on the number, the second note up on the "+", down on the next number and up on the next "+". Keep it steady. There is very little time between eighth notes. They go as fast as you can count and sometimes faster. Tap your foot while you are counting. Notice that your foot goes down on the numbered beat and up on the "+" beat. Your right hand moves the same way. Practice eighth notes while counting and tapping your foot.

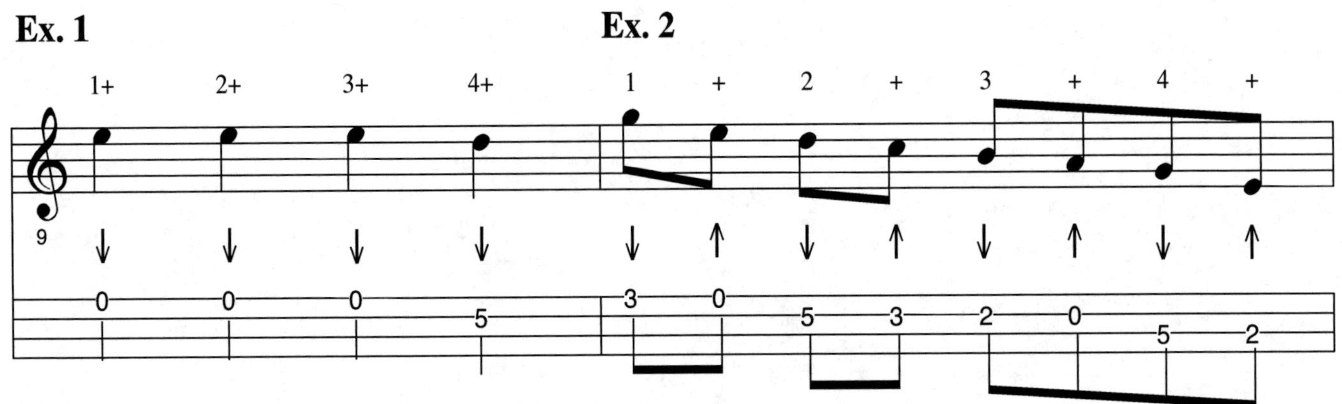

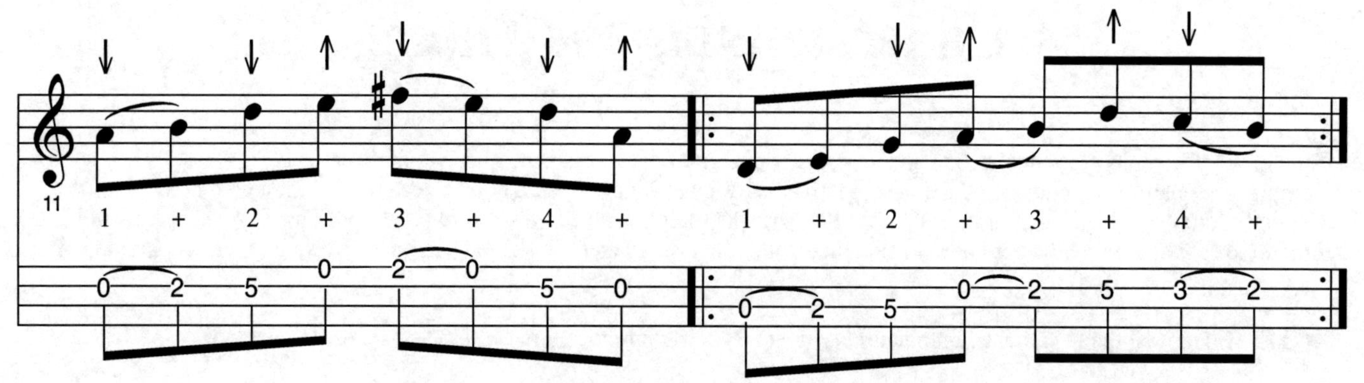
11
1 + 2 + 3 + 4 + 1 + 2 + 3 + 4 +
0 2 5 0 2 0 5 0 0 2 5 0 2 5 3 2

Understanding the Timing

Playing Hornpipes

The timing of hornpipes, even though comprised mostly of eightht notes, is a little different than the reels. Hornpipes are played with the feel of a dotted eighth note followed by a sixteenth note instead of straight eighth notes. The first example of Alexander's Hornpipe is written with the timing denoted how it is to be played. This looks awkward and difficult to read so I wrote the hornpipes in straight eighth note fashion (see the second version or Alexander's Hornpipe) in order to make it a little easier to read.

NOTE: Though written in straight eighth notes be sure to try to capture the dotted eighth and sixteenth note feel.

Alexander's Hornpipe

Example of dotted eighth notes and sixteenth notes

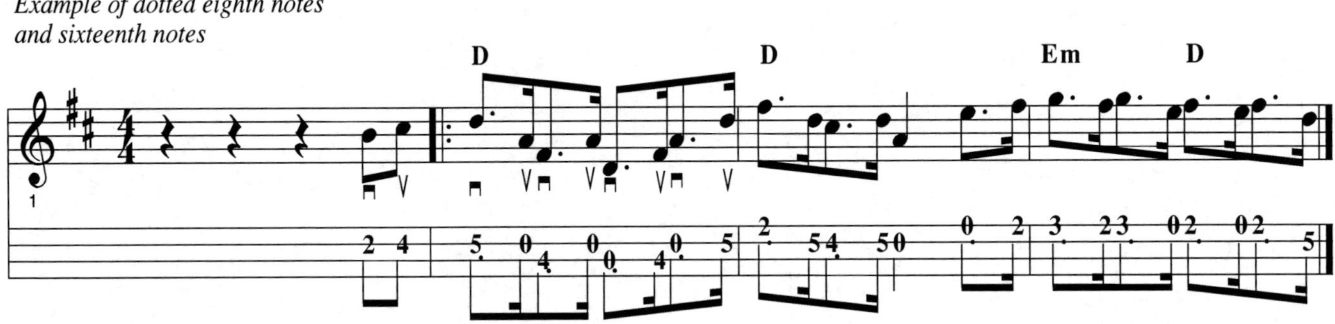

Alexander's Hornpipe

Example of Hornpipes written in this book.: Straight eighth notes to be played as dotted eighths and sixteenths (see above).

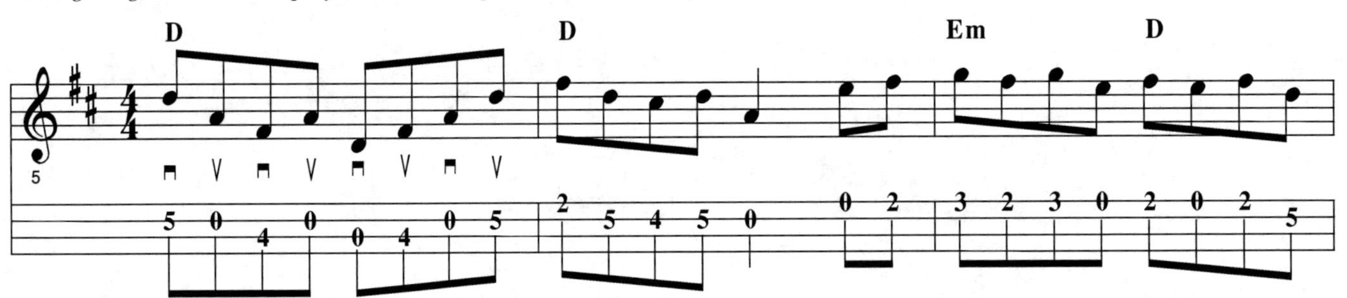

Jigs

Jigs are played differently with the picking hand because the beats are different than those of hornpipes and reels. Jigs are written in 6/8 time which means that there are 6 beats in the measure and the eighth note get a full beat. They play and sound like DA da da DA da da. Usually grouped in two sets three's. Be sure to accent the first note of the three.

Notice the down up marks in the measures on the next page. You will see some down up down down up down sets and you will see down up down up down up sets. You will have to make the call what you do with the right hand. As they say "it doesn't matter" as long as you get the notes in time.

NOTE: Do Not Play Like - down down down down up up. This would be incorrect. You will want to get an alternating picking pattern with the picking hand in order to achieve the speed required.

Apples In Winter

Examples of two different picking practices with jigs.

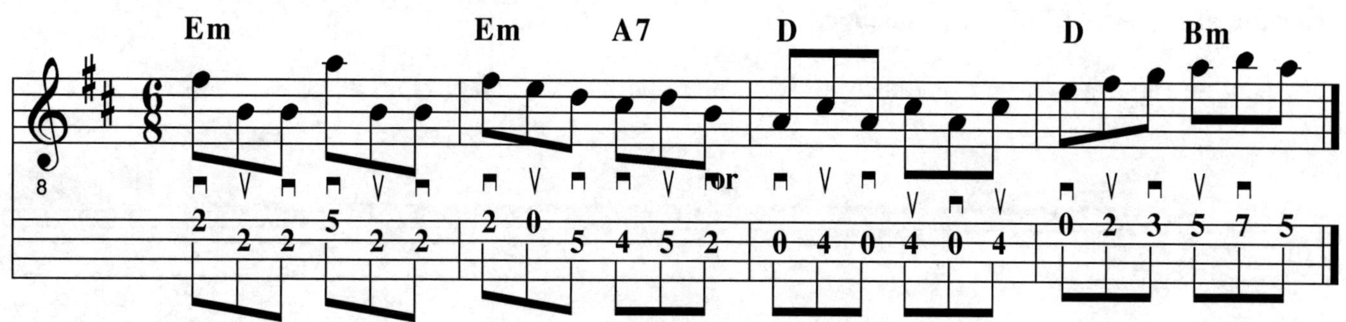

Waltzes

Waltzes comprize some of the most beautiful music written. Unfortunately I could only get a handful in this collection but be looking for more in the future. The waltzes can be pretty plain unless you know a simple way to dress them up. The following two lines illustrate one demonastration.

First learn the tune as written in the book. Then try this. Strum the chord written for the measure from bass to treble to the melody note but not going past the melody note. This technique will accentuate the melody without burying it. If the melody note is note generally found in the chord, you will have to hold the melody note and the remainder of the chord (see the "G" measure in the last line).

Maid Of Glenconnel

Maid Of Glenconnel

Jigs

There are three variations of the jig: **The Double Jig** in 6/8 time, **The Single Jig** in 6/8 or 12/8 time and the **Hop Jig** - also called a **Slip Jig** in 9/8 time.

The **Double Jig** is delineated from other jigs by its characteristic rhythm of repeated eighth notes:

At the player's discretion, repeated eighth notes may also be interpreted with a dotted eighth and sixteenth note rhythm.

The A and B sections of the **Double Jig** will use the running eighth note figure predominantly throughout with the last measure changing to:

The **Single Jig** incorporates more of the Quarter note eighth note combinations

The last bar or measure of a section often ends on a final dotted quater and quarter note combination.

The **Slip Jig** or Hop Jig uses various groupings of eighth notes, quater notes and dotted quarter notes.

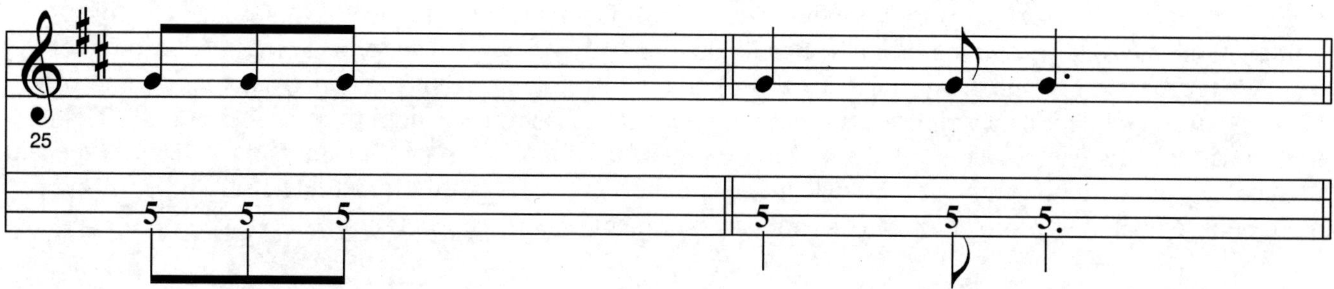

Hornpipes

The **Hornpipe** is played at a slower tempo than a reel and in a more heavily accented fashion.
It is customary for the closing measures of each section in a hornpipe to end with a quarter note set.

The dotted eighth/sixteenth rhythm usually prevails in the performance of the hornpipe.
It is frequently notated as a pattern of straight eighth notes.
The Hornpipe may also be distinguished by it's formal structure. While it is often a two-part (AB) form, extended forms like ABC, ABCD, AABA etc. may differentiate it from the reel.

Reels

The **Reel** is the most popular genre of tunes played by traditional instrumentalists. It is often played at a fast tempo, consequently is appeals to the virtuoso player. Strings of repeated eighth notes are often associated with the reel.

Suggested Rolls

Rolls occur when you have a quarter note and you wish to add a bit of flair to the note and song. The first note written in the measures below represent the note to be replaced by the roll. The roll is a five note set of notes that take one beat to execute. In most cases you will hit the first note of the five and then hammer-on/pull-off/hammer-on and then hit the last note on an up swing. Practice these roll sets until they smooth out. The Celtic fiddles will tell you that you don't really need to hear all of the notes in the roll. It is more a passage of time and a sound that occurs in the music at times when you feel the song needs a little something else. These rolls are often replaced with just a triplet. Practice them and enter them into the songs as desired.

9
11
13
15

Track 1
The Cinderella Waltz
Arr. by Steve Kaufman
Key of G

Track 2
Cupid's Waltz
Key of G
Arr. by Steve Kaufman
G G D7 G
G G D7 G G
G C D7 G G
C D7 G D G
D G G C D7 G

Track 3

Drink Your Tea, Love

Key of G

Arr. by Steve Kaufman

G
G
D7
G
17
G
G
D
G
21
D7
G
D7
G
25
G
G
D7
G
29

Track 4

The Maid of Glenconnel

Key of D

Arr. by Steve Kaufman

A7
D
D
E7
20
0 3 0 5 4 0 5 5 5 2 2 0 0
A7
D
D
24
0 2 3 5 2 5 5 2 5
A7
A7
D
27
0 4 0 0 2 5 4 0 5
A7
D
D
30
0 5 0 2 5 5 5

My Lodging's on the Cold Ground
Track 5
Believe Me, If All Those Endearing Young Charms
Arr. by Steve Kaufman
Key of G
G G
C C G
D G D7 G
G7 C C
G D7 G G

G G C C
17
2 5 3 3 5 0 3 3 3 2 0
G D G D
21
5 3 2 0 5 0 2 5 2 0 2 0
G G7 C C
25
5 0 5 5 2 5 3 0 3 3 2 0
G D G G
29
5 3 2 0 5 0 5 5

Track 6

Over the Moor

Key of D

Arr. by Steve Kaufman

Track 7
The Pirate's Waltz
Key of D
Arr. by Steve Kaufman
D G A7
D D G A7
D D D G
Em A7 D Em
A7 D D

Track 8
The Shepherd's Wife
Arr. by Steve Kaufman
Key of G
G G G
G C G Am
D7 G G G
G C D7 G
G G D7 Em

Bm
C
G
A7
20
D7
G
D7
24
Em
Bm
C
27
D7
G
G
30

Track 9

The Wild Hills O' Wannie's

Key of Am

Arr. by Steve Kaufman

G
G
G
3
21
3
2
3
5
0
2
3
3
5
3
2
3
G
Am
Am
24
5
2
3
5
4
5
0
2
3
Am
3
Am
Em
27
3
5
7
5
4
5
0
0
2
3
2
0
G
3
Am
Am
30
3
5
0
5
2
5
0
0
0
0

Track 10

The American Dwarf

Key of D

The Frost Is All Over

Arr. by Steve Kaufman

 Track 11

Apples in Winter

General White's, The Misfortunate Rake, Rattle the Quilt
The Shamrock, Next Sunday Is My Wedding Day

Arr. by Steve Kaufman

Key of Em

Em Em A7 D

5 4 2 2 2 5 2 2 2 0 5 4 5 2 0 4 0 4 0 4

D Bm Em G

4

0 2 4 5 0 5 2 2 2 2 0 2 5 0 2 3 2 3

D Bm Em Em

7

1 2

2 0 5 2 0 4 5 2 2 2 5 4 5 2 2 2 5 2

Em Em D

10

0 2 0 0 5 2 3 2 0 2 5 2 5 0 5 5 0 4

D Bm C G

13

0 4 0 5 0 2 0 2 0 0 5 2 5 0 2 3 5

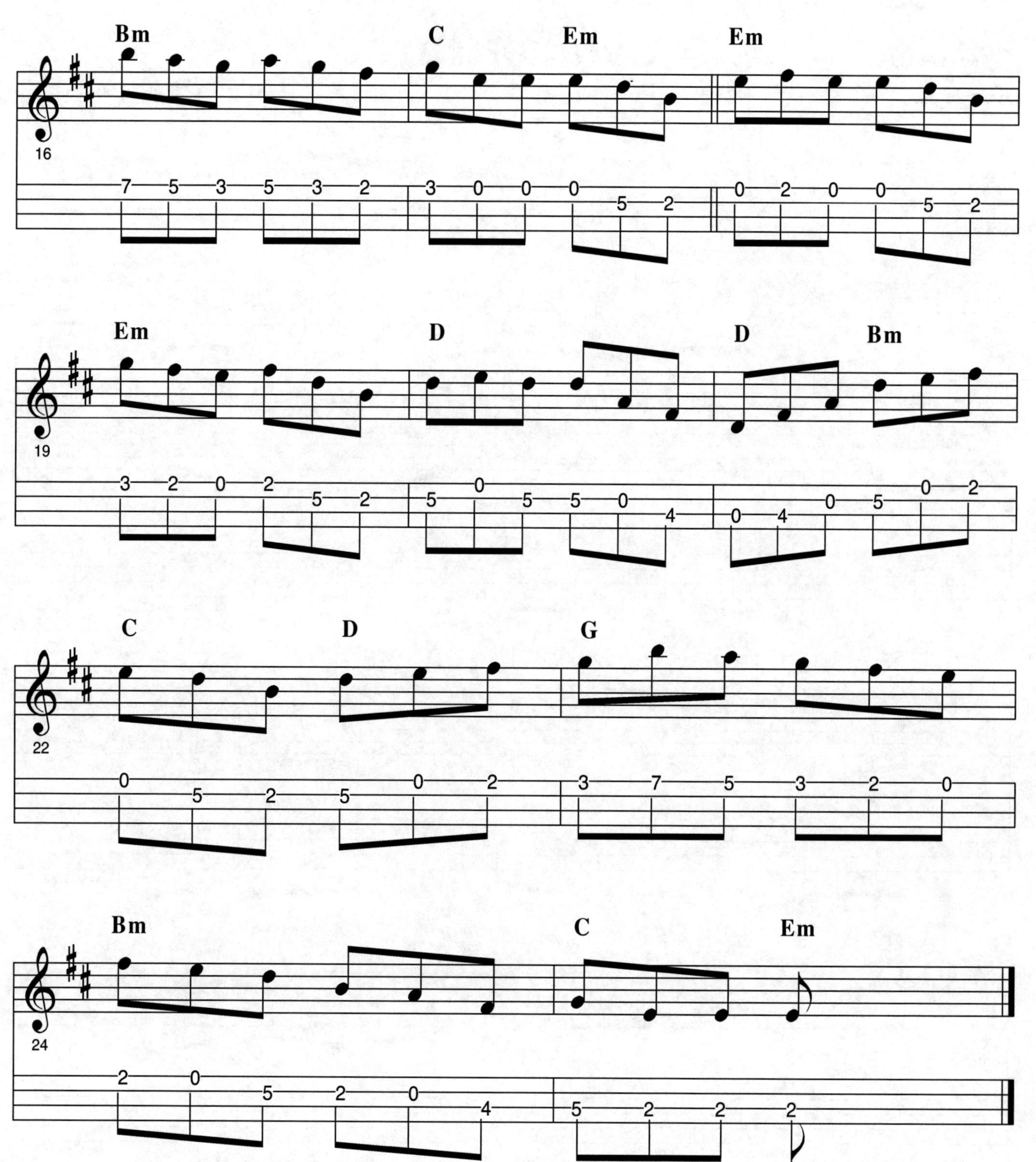
Bm
C
Em
Em
16
7 5 3 5 3 2
3 0 0 0 5 2
0 2 0 0 5 2
Em
D
D
Bm
19
3 2 0 2 5 2
5 0 5 5 0 4
0 4 0 5 0 2
C
D
G
22
0 5 2 5 0 2
3 7 5 3 2 0
Bm
C
Em
24
2 0 5 2 0 4
5 2 2 2

Track 12

Bank of Turf

Key of D

Arr. by Steve Kaufman

Barbary Bell

Track 13

Key of G St. Patrick's Day Arr. by Steve Kaufman

Cherish the Ladies

Track 14

Key of D

Capper's Jig Humours Of Cappa

Arr. by Steve Kaufman

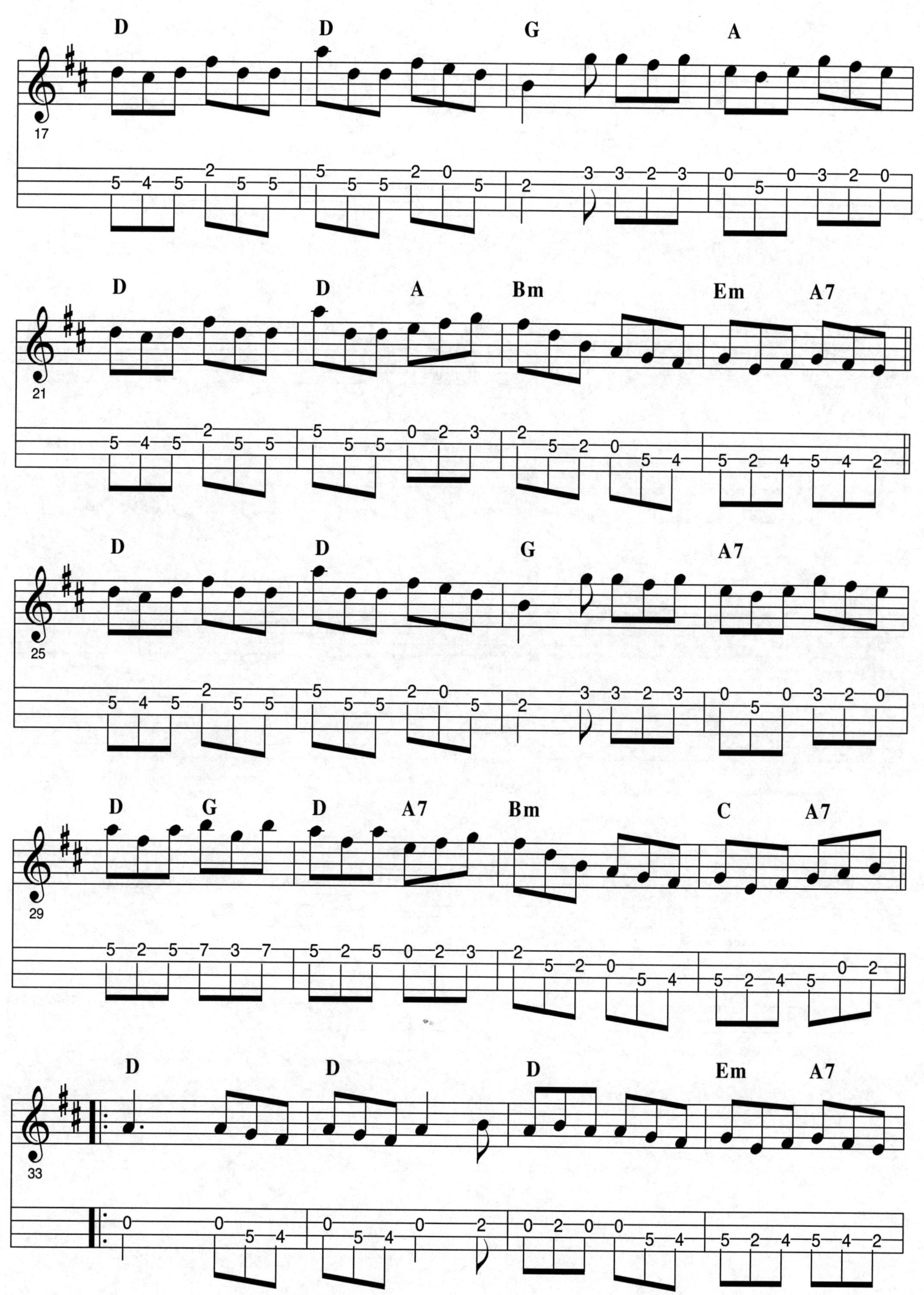
D D G A
D D A Bm Em A7
D D G A7
D G D A7 Bm C A7
D D D Em A7

D
D
G
C
Em
A7
1
37
Em
A7
2
D
D
D
41
C
A7
D
D
45
G
C
Em
A7
D.S.
48

Coleman's Cross

Track 15

Key of Em

Kimmel's No. 2

Arr. by Steve Kaufman

Track 16
Drops of Drink
Arr. by Steve Kaufman
Key of G
G
G
Am
Am
D7
G
G
Am
Em
Em
Em
D
Em
Em
Em
D
Em
G
Am
Em
Em

Track 17

The Fair-Haired Boy

The Boys From Carrickroe The Kerryman's Rambles
The Last Of The Lot

Arr. by Steve Kaufman

Key of Am

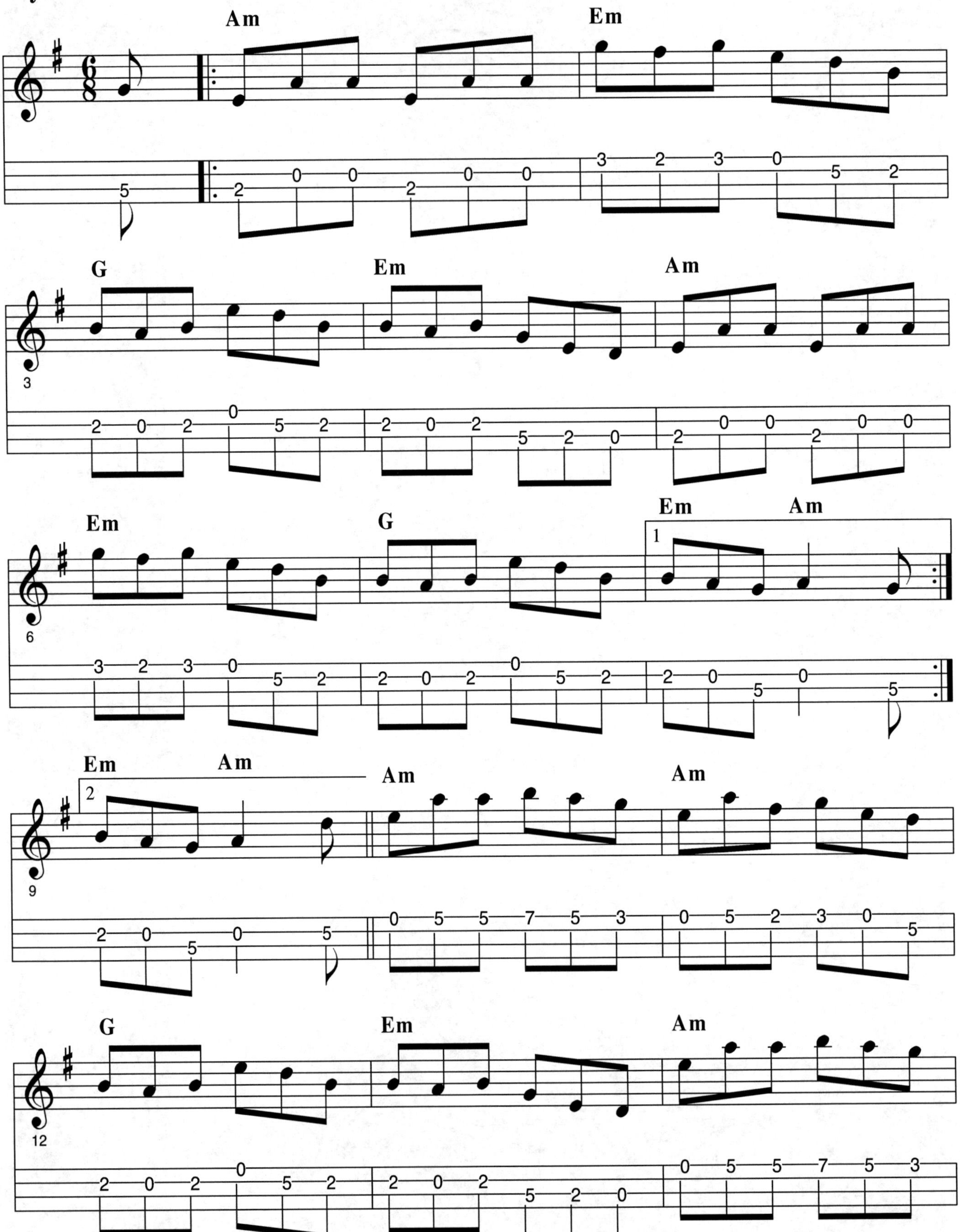
Am
Em
G
Em
Am
Em
G
Em
Am
1
Em
Am
2
Am
Am
G
Em
Am

Am
G
Em
Am
15
Am
Am
G
18
Em
Am
Em
21
G
Em
Am
24

The Geese in the Bog

Track 18

Key of C

Arr. by Steve Kaufman

Track 19
The Gobby-O
Key of Am
Arr. by Steve Kaufman
Am Am G
G Am Am Am Em
Am Am Am Em
D C G Am Am
Am Em Am Am

Happy to Meet and Sorry to Part

Track 20

My Love In The Morning The Wake Jig
Winston At The Glenville Hall

Arr. by Steve Kaufman

Key of G

G C G Em Em C

G C G Em D G C

G C D G Bm C D

Em C D G

A7 D G G C

Track 21
Haste to the Wedding
Key of D
Arr. by Steve Kaufman
D G D D
A7 D G D D A7
D D D G
D Em A7 D G D
D A7 D D

Track 22
The Humours of Ballyloughlin
The Hurler's March
Arr. by Steve Kaufman
Key of G

D C C D D
20
C C D D C
25
C D C D C C A D
30
D D A A7 D
35
D A7 D G D G D
40
1
2

Track 23

The Irish Washerwoman

Key of G

Arr. by Steve Kaufman

Track 24

Katie's Rambles

Key of D

The Heart Of My Kitty

Arr. by Steve Kaufman

Track 25
Knocknagow
Key of Am
Arr. by Steve Kaufman

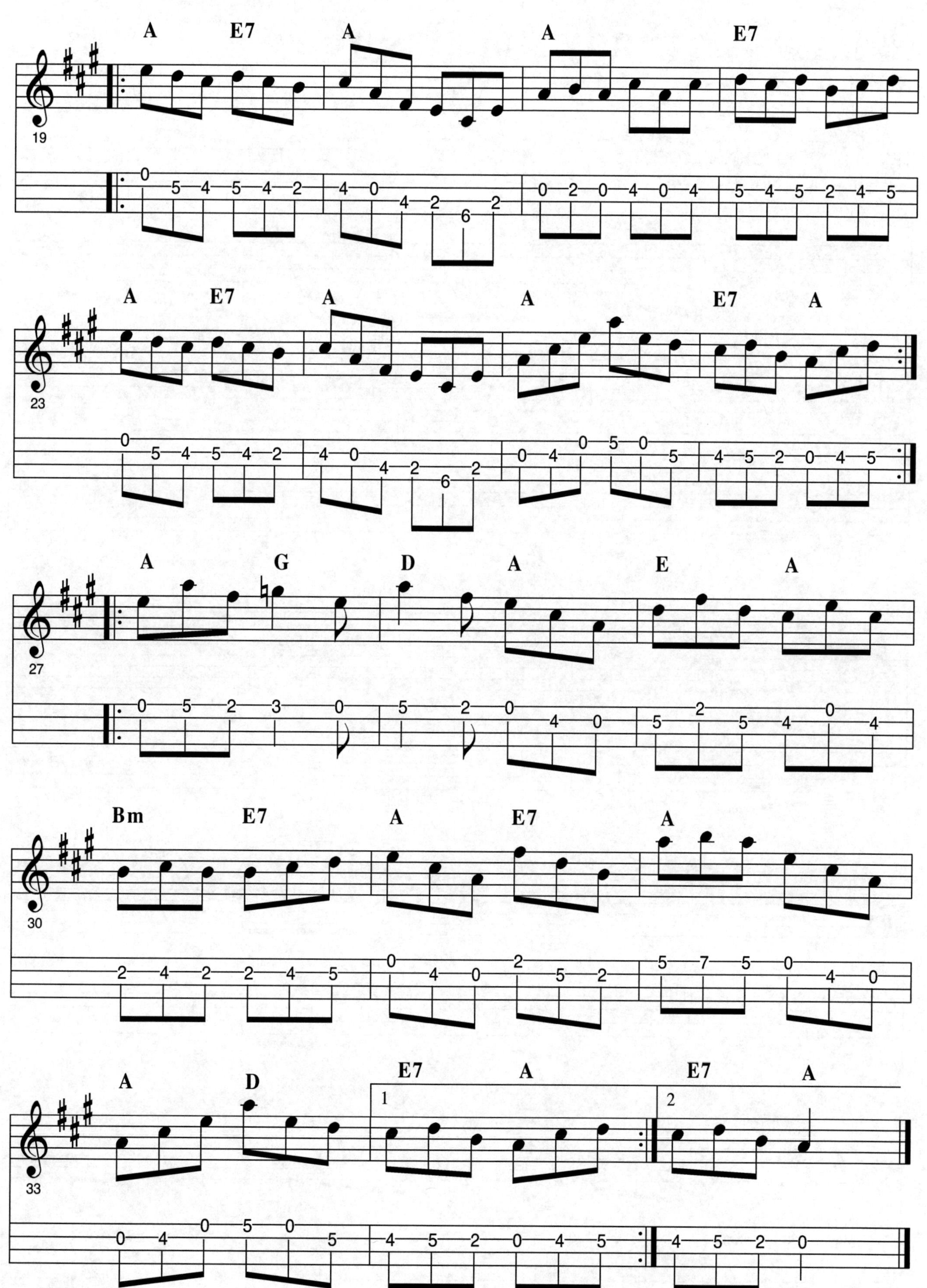
A E7 A A E7
19
A E7 A A E7 A
23
A G D A E A
27
Bm E7 A E7 A
30
A D E7 A E7 A
33
1
2

Track 26
Lady Douglas Mary
Arr. by Steve Kaufman
Key of D
D G A D
E7 A D G D
D A7 D D
D D A
A D G Em A

D
A7
D
16
G
A7
D
E7
A7
19
D
G
D
22
D
A7
D
24

Track 27

The Lady in the Boat

The Bugle Quickstep

Arr. by Steve Kaufman

Key of D

Track 28
Lannigan's Ball
Key of Em
Arr. by Steve Kaufman
Em Em D
D Em Em Bm Em Am
Em Em Em D
Em Bm Em D
Em Am Em Em

Track 29
Maggie Brown
Key of G
Arr. by Steve Kaufman

D
G
D
Em
D
A7
13
0
4
0
0
5
7
3
7
5
2
5
0
2
3
3
2
0
2
5
2
3
0
4
D
G
C
G
C
G
17
5
5
5
0
1
0
3
0
5
2
5
3
5
3
2
3
2
C
G
D7
G
C
20
0
3
0
5
2
5
4
0
4
0
2
4
5
0
2
2
4
5
Am
D
G
D
G
23
0
2
3
5
0
2
3
5
2
3
0
4
5
5

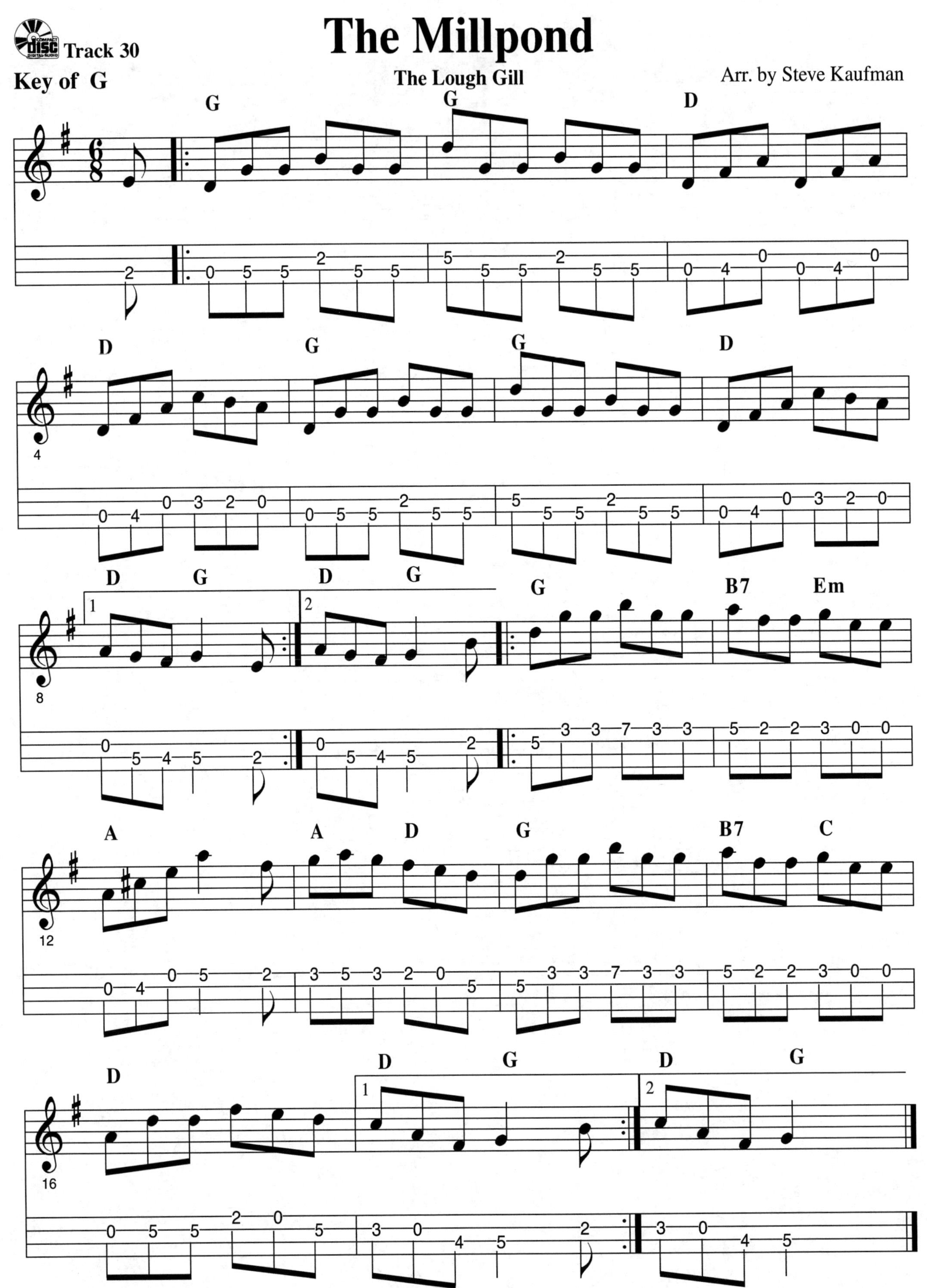
Track 30
The Millpond
Key of G
The Lough Gill
Arr. by Steve Kaufman
G
G
D
D
G
G
D
4
D
G
D
G
G
B7
Em
8
A
A
D
G
B7
C
12
D
D
G
D
G
16

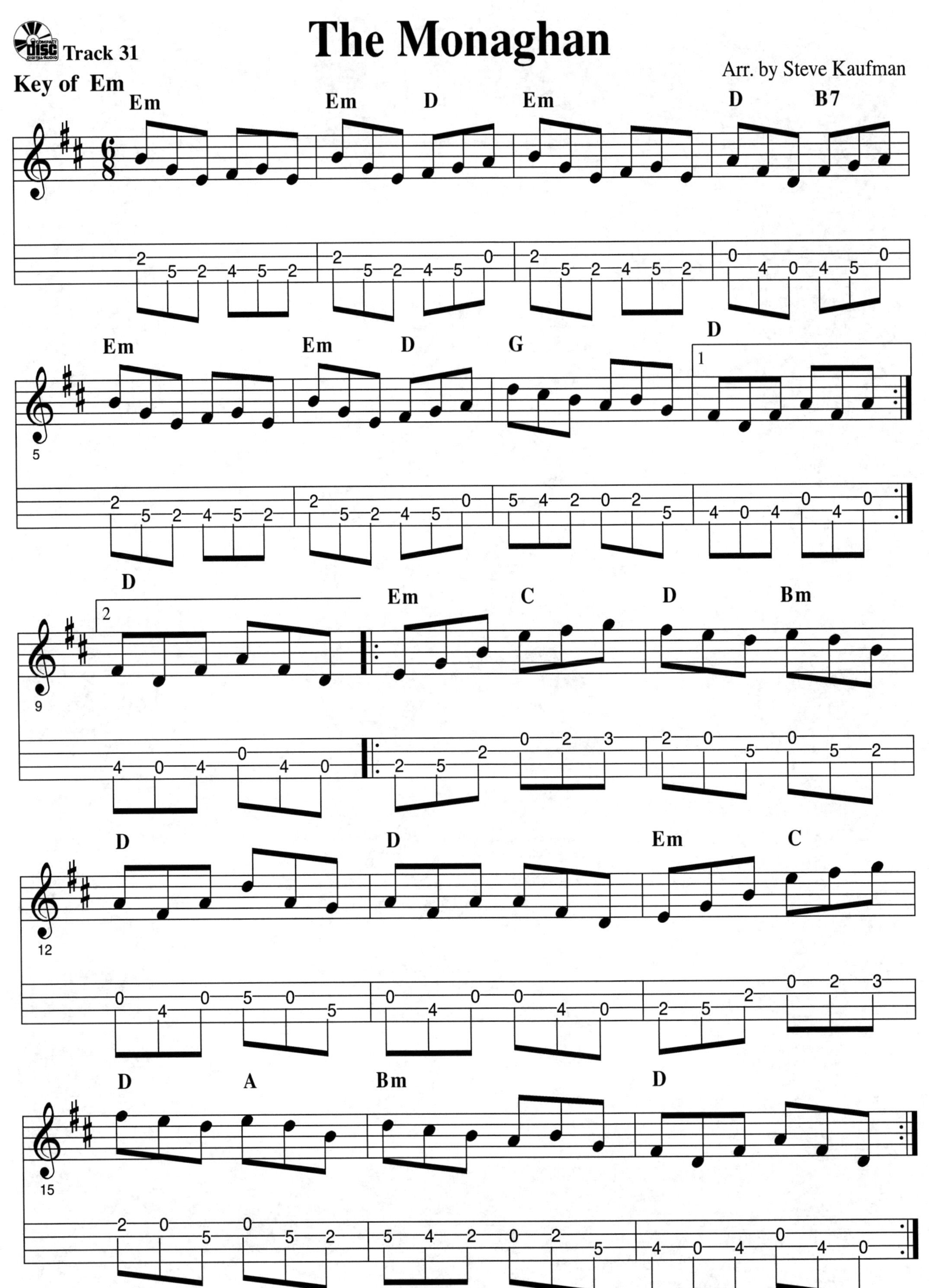
Track 31
The Monaghan
Arr. by Steve Kaufman
Key of Em
Em Em D Em D B7
Em Em D G D
D Em C D Bm
D D Em C
D A Bm D

Em
Em
Em
A7
D
18
Em
Em
Bm
D
22
Em
Em
D
Em
D
26
Em
Em
Bm
D
D
30
1
2

Track 32

Muckin' O' Geordie's Byre

Arr. by Steve Kaufman

Key of D

My Wife's a Wanton Wee Thing

Arr. by Steve Kaufman

D
A7
D
D
16
2 5 2 0 4 0
5 5 2 3
5 7 5 2 5 2
D
C
C
19
5 7 5 2 5 2
3 5 3 0 3 0
3 5 3 0 3 0
D
D
G
22
5 7 5 2 5 2
5 7 5 3 5 7
D
A7
D
24
2 3 5 3 0 4
5 5

Track 34

Off She Goes

Key of D

Arr. by Steve Kaufman

Track 35

The Old Grey Goose

Key of G

We'll All Take A Coach And Trip It Away

Arr. by Steve Kaufman

G D Em
D D G B7
Em C G D Em
G G Am Am
G C G D Em Em

Em Bm C D D
18
Em Bm A G D Em Em
22
G D Em G D G B7
27
Em A G D Em Em
32
G D C G D
36

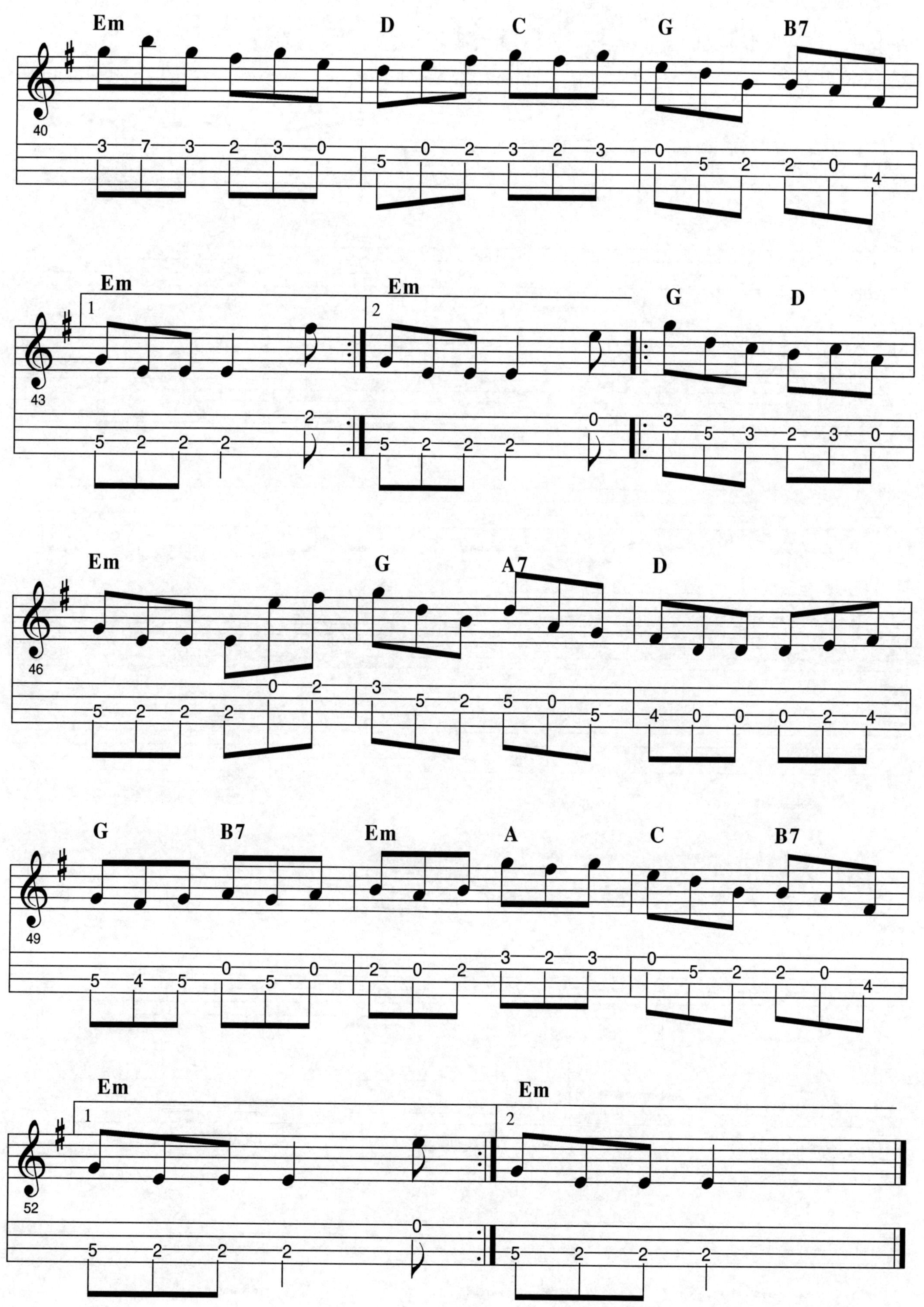
Em
D
C
G
B7
40
Em
1
Em
2
G
D
43
Em
G
A7
D
46
G
B7
Em
A
C
B7
49
Em
1
Em
2
52

Track 36

Old Hag, You Have Killed Me

Key of G

Stop, Old Hag, Or You'll Kill Me

Arr. by Steve Kaufman

Track 37
Old Rosin, The Beau
Key of G
Arr. by Steve Kaufman

Track 38

Paddy O' Rafferty

Key of D

Drink This Cup

Arr. by Steve Kaufman

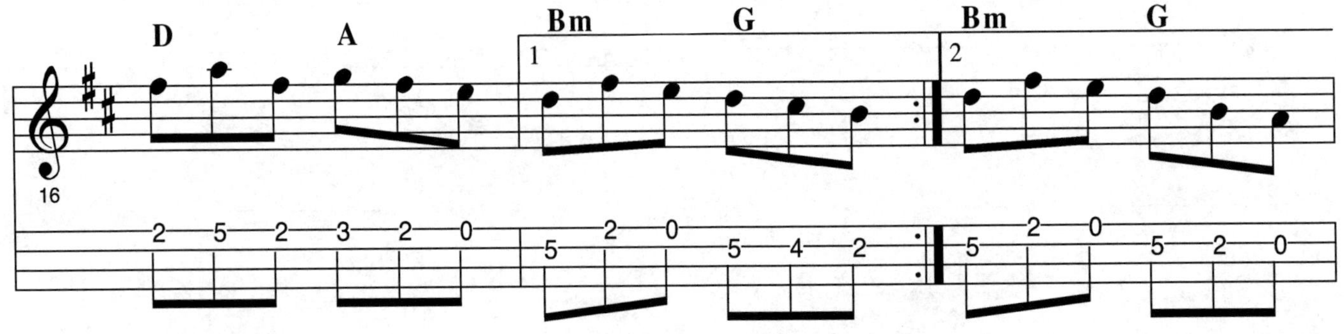

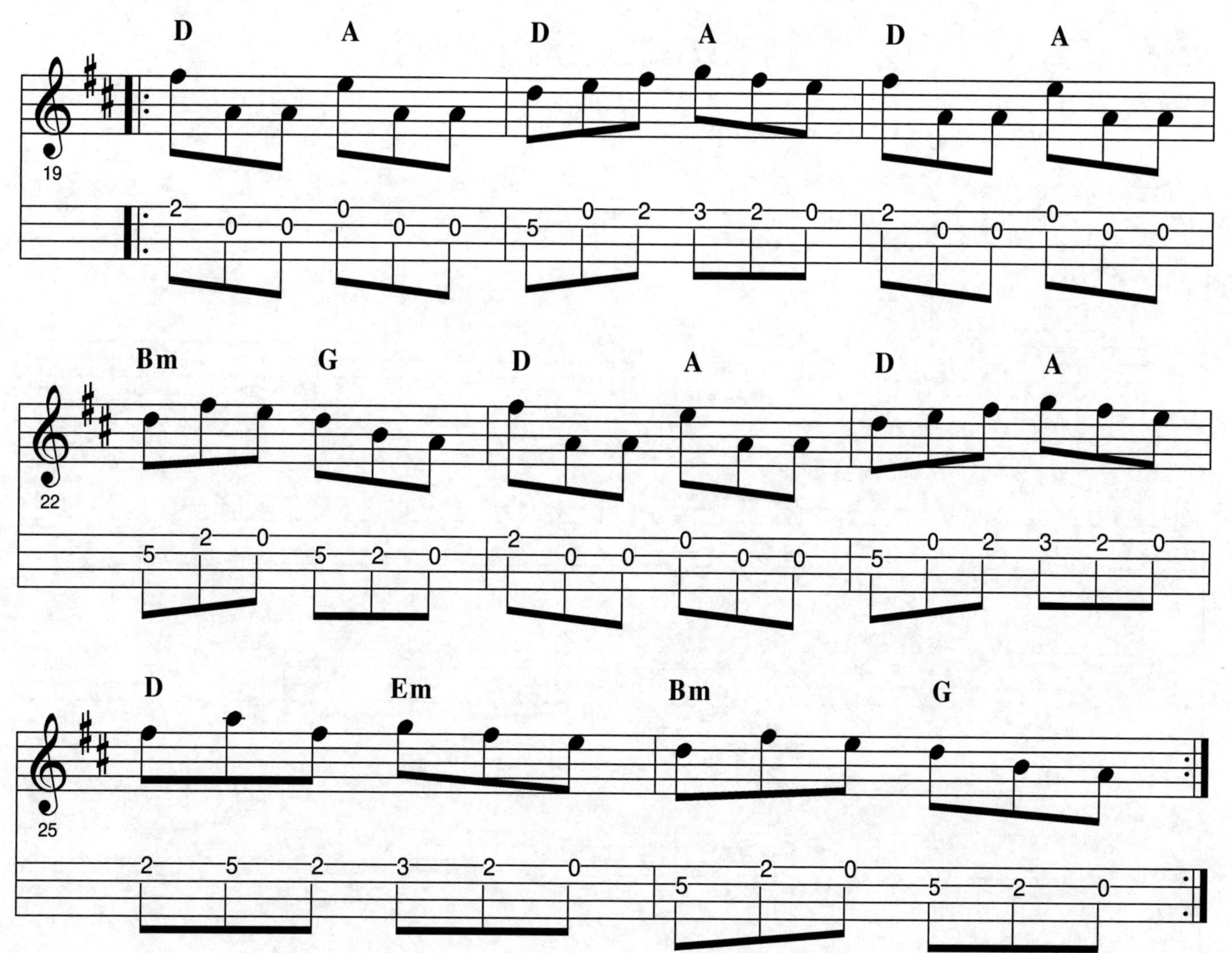
D
A
D
A
D
A
19
Bm
G
D
A
D
A
22
D
Em
Bm
G
25

Track 39
Plymouth Lasses
The Sylph
Key of D
Arr. by Steve Kaufman

Track 40

Queen of The Fair

Arr. by Steve Kaufman

Key of D

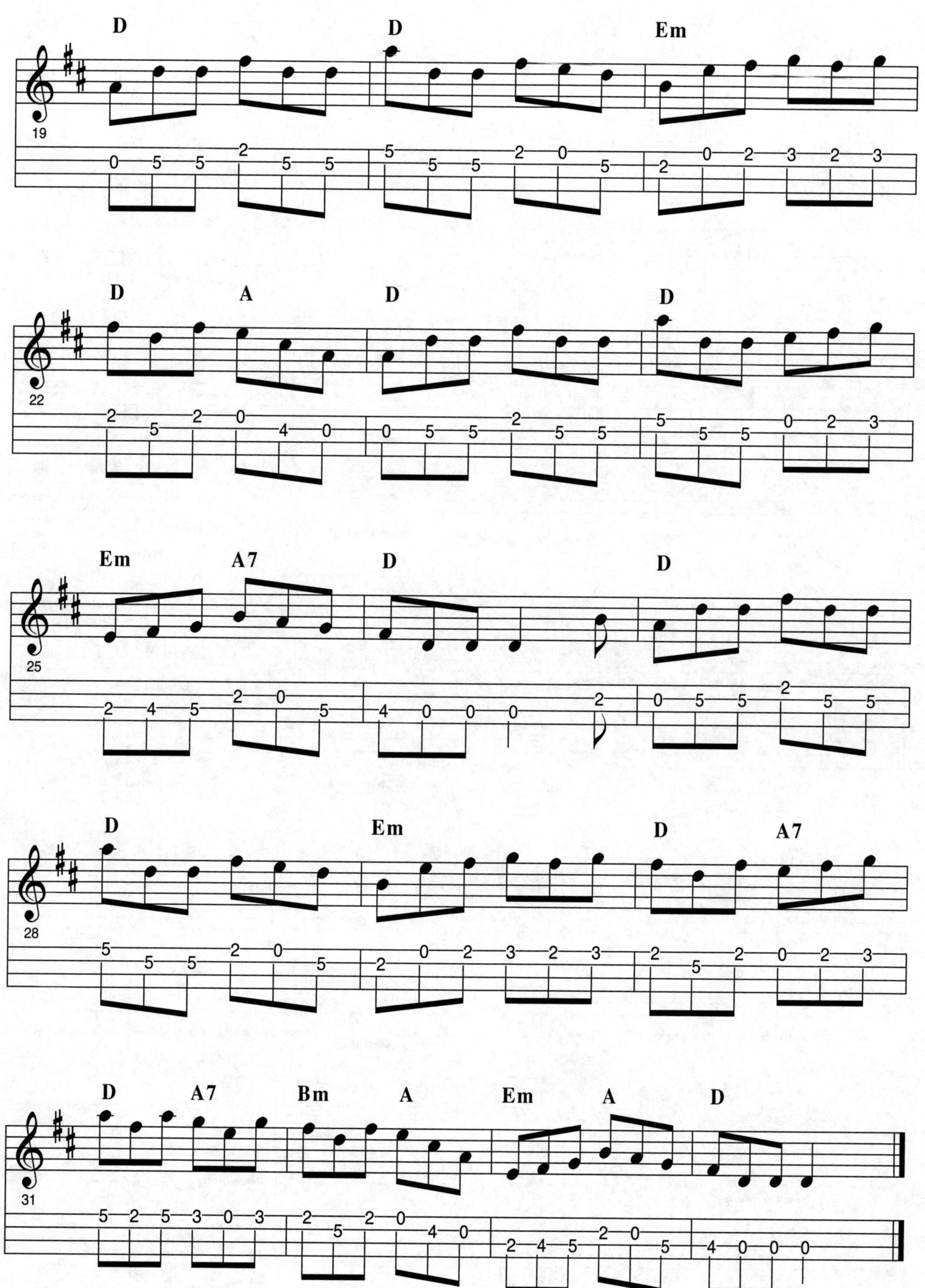
19
D D Em
22
D A D D
25
Em A7 D D
28
D Em D A7
31
D A7 Bm A Em A D

Track 41
The Rollicking Irishman
Yorkshire Lasses
Key of D
Arr. by Steve Kaufman
D G A7 D A7
D A7 D G A7 D A7
D D D A
E7 A7 D G A7
D A7 D D

Track 42
Rose in the Heather
Key of D
Arr. by Steve Kaufman

Track 43
The Swallow's Nest
Key of Am
The Dancing Master
Dromey's Fancy
Arr. by Steve Kaufman
Am Am G
G Am Am F Em G
Am Am Am Am
Am D G Am Am D
Em G Am Am

Track 44

Tar Road to Sligo

Key of D

Arr. by Steve Kaufman

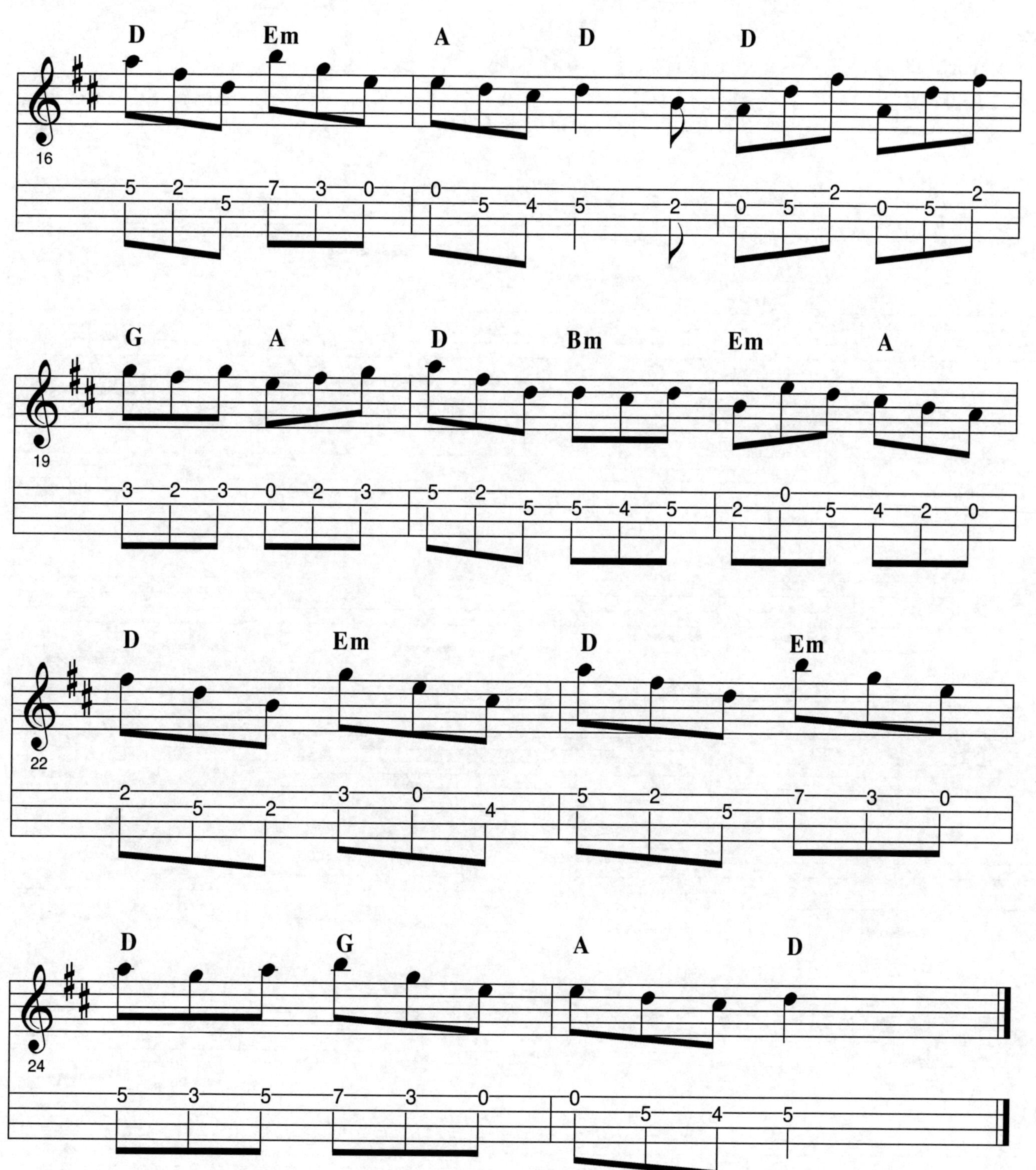
D
Em
A
D
D
16
G
A
D
Bm
Em
A
19
D
Em
D
Em
22
D
G
A
D
24

 Track 45

Tatter Jack Walsh

Key of D

Father Jack Walsh **Kitty Of Bullinamore**
To Cashel I'm Going

Arr. by Steve Kaufman

SCOTLAND

Track 46
The Three Sea Captains
Arr. by Steve Kaufman
Key of G
G Am D7 G
4
G C G
7
Am D7 G
10
Am D7 G G
13
C D7 G Em C D G

G C D G A7 D
17
C Am G Em Am
21
D7 G Am D
24
G G C Am
27
G Em C D G
30

Track 47

Trip to the Cottage

Key of G

Arr. by Steve Kaufman

Track 48
Tripping Upstairs
Key of D
Arr. by Steve Kaufman

Track 49

The Wandering Minstrel

The Dandy Scholar The Fair Maidens Merry Maidens
Michael Coleman's Willy Walsh

Key of D

Arr. by Steve Kaufman

G
G
G
3
21
3
2
3
5
0
2
3
3
5
3
2
3
G
Am
Am
24
5
2
3
5
4
5
0
2
3
Am
3
Am
Em
27
3
5
7
5
4
5
0
0
2
3
2
0
G
3
Am
Am
30
3
0
5
5
2
5
0
0
0
0

About the Author

Steve Kaufman was born into a musical family in 1957. His father was a jazz piano player and his mother was a classically trained pianist. Music was always around. At age four, Steve started plinking at the piano, and did so for several years. At age ten, he moved on to the electric guitar, but put it away after a few years. Next came the cello for a few years, starting in the fifth grade. After this, Steve picked up the acoustic guitar and blazed right through a "Folk Guitar" method book. When finished, he thought *...if this is as hard as it gets, its not for him.* Then, his younger brother Will started playing the banjo, and Will's instructor told him he needed a rhythm guitar player to help with his timing. Steve picked up his guitar again, and got into the bluegrass rhythm. One day Will brought home a Flatt and Scruggs LP which featured Doc Watson on guitar, and Steve was hooked on flatpicking.

Steve practiced hard with his newfound love of music, sometimes up to eight hours a day. At age 18, he entered the National Flatpicking Championships in Winfield, Kansas, and made the top ten. The following year was a wash, but in 1977, Steve took second place to Mark O'Conner. In 1978 at age 21, he returned to win the championship. After being barred for five years, he returned on the sixth year to win the 1984 championships again. At the time, Winfield barred the winner for five years, but they could come back on the sixth year. In 1986 they decided to open up the contest to everyone and not bar the past years champs. Steve returned to win his goal. He became the winner and the first and (as of this writing) only three-time winner of the National Flatpicking Championships. He is also noted to have three consecutive wins in the nationals, because he was barred all the years he did not enter.

Steve continues to work hard in the world of music. He began producing books and videos in 1989 after teaching private lessons for close to 20 years. His catalog of instructional materials is close to 44 items and his listening CDs and videos number over 14. Steve began touring the world, conducting seminars, workshops, clinics and concerts in 1990. After five years, he and his wife Donna began *Steve Kaufman's Flatpicking Camp.* Every other year they have added more camps into their agenda, and now, under the title *Steve Kaufman's Acoustic Kamps,* they host a *Fingerpicking Kamp,* and an *Old Time Banjo, Bluegrass Banjo and Mandolin Kamp.* They have grown into the largest kamps of their kind in the world, with students traveling from around the world to Maryville, Tennessee. In 2002, 2004 and 2006 Steve Kaufman received the Gold Award from a reader's poll in *Acoustic Guitar Magazine* for running the "Best Workshops, Seminars and Camps."

Steve stays busy being a husband and father, running his Kamps, tour schedule, writing books and recording videos and CDs. He also owns and operates the area's premier acoustic venue and espresso bar: *The Palace Theater* in downtown Maryville (see www.palacetheater.com). Also connected to the Palace Theater is a café and deli called *The Palace Café and Catering.*

Steve Kaufman's Instructional Materials also at www.flatpik.com

Kaufman's Favorite Fifty Celtic Hornpipes for Flatpicking Guitar Book and CD

Kaufman's Favorite Fifty Celtic Jigs and Waltzes for Flatpicking Guitar Book and CD

Kaufman's Favorite Fifty Celtic Reels A through L for Flatpicking Guitar Book and CD

Kaufman's Favorite Fifty Celtic Reels L through W for Flatpicking Guitar Book and CD

Classic Arrangements to Vintage Songs - Book with 2 CDs

Band in the Book for Bluegrass Vocals - Book with CD

Band in the Book for Bluegrass Instrumentals - Book with CD

Band in the Book for Gospel Vocals - Book with CD

Bullet Train - The Book with Full CD

Kaufman's Collection Of Traditional American Fiddle Tunes Book and 2 CDs

Kaufman's Collection Of Traditional American Fiddle Tunes DVD

Flatpicking The Gospels for Guitar Book with CD and DVD

Flatpicking The Rags and Polkas - Book w/ 2 CDs

Championship Flatpicking Book with CD and DVD

You Can Teach Yourself Flatpicking Guitar with CD or DVD

The Complete Flatpicking Book with CD and DVD

Smokey Mountain Christmas For Guitar - Book with CD

The Power Flatpicking Fingerboard Book with CD and DVD

Blazing Guitar Solos for One or More Book with CD

The Legacy Of Doc Watson - Book

The Anthology of Norman Blake - Book

Flatpicking Banjo Tunes for Guitar - DVD with Booklet

Figuring Out The Fingerboard for Guitar - DVD with Booklet

Learn to Play Waltzes Flatpicking Style - Video with Booklet

4-Hour Celtic Workout Book with 4 CDs

Picking Up Speed - DVD with Booklet - Drills for Flatpicking Guitarists

Flatpicking Through The Holidays! - VHS Video with Booklet

Lead Breaks to Bluegrass Songs Flatpicking Style - Video

Flatpicking With Doc (and Steve) - DVD with Booklet

The Art Of Crosspicking - DVD with Booklet

Learn To Flatpick 1, 2, 3 - 3 DVD Set - Beginner, Intermediate and Advanced with Booklets

Easy Gospel Guitar - DVD with Booklet

Basic Bluegrass Rhythm Guitar - DVD with Booklet

4 Hr. Bluegrass Workout - Book with 4 CD

Flatpicking The Gospels for Mandolin Book w/CD - Audio

Kaufman's Favorite Fifty Celtic Hornpipes for Mandolin Book and CD

Kaufman's Favorite Fifty Celtic Jigs and Waltzes for Mandolin Book and CD

Kaufman's Favorite Fifty Celtic Reels A through L for Mandolin - Book and CD

Kaufman's Favorite Fifty Celtic Reels L through W for Mandolin - Book and CD

Blazing Mandolin Solos for One or More - Book with CD

Smokey Mountain Christmas For Mandolin - Book with CD

20 Bluegrass Mandolin Solos That Every Parking Lot Picker Should Know Vol. 1 Book with/ 6 CDs

20 Bluegrass Mandolin Solos That Every Parking Lot Picker Should Know Vol. 2 Book with/ 6 CDs

20 Bluegrass Guitar Solos That Every Parking Lot Picker Should Know Vol. 1 Book with/ 6 CDs

20 Bluegrass Guitar Solos That Every Parking Lot Picker Should Know Vol. 2 Book with/ 6 CDs

20 Bluegrass Guitar Solos That Every Parking Lot Picker Should Know Vol. 3 Book with/ 6 CDs

20 Bluegrass Guitar Solos That Every Parking Lot Picker Should Know Vol. 4 Book with/ 6 CDs

20 Swing Tunes Guitar Solos That Every Parking Lot Picker Should Know - Book with 6 CDs

20 Gospel Songs Every Parking Lot Picker Should Know - Book with 6 CDs

4 Hr. Bluegrass Workout for Banjo - Book with 4 CDs